21

MW00778188

I look forward to
when you sign a copy
of your book for me.—

all the best—

Elea...

too

much

beauty

eleanor seigler

Copyright © 2018 Eleanor Seigler

All Rights Reserved
ISBN-13: 978-0692194348
ISBN-10: 0692194347

for so many

The last several years revolved around trying to find a home and to secure work. What happened, instead, was that I came face to face with humanity and all of the humans in it in ways I had not yet before known. In what simultaneously became a journey to find and better understand myself as a person in the world, I instead had the privilege of losing myself and gaining the rest of the world in its place, myself included. The man said no to me, but the People said yes.

song suggestion: *Opening*, Trevor Oswalt, East Forest

I can only speak to my experience of life. I will do my best to convey.

too

much

beauty

First off, I find you to be quite beautiful.

I am not sure we would be here if we were not supposed to just be.

Everything up to now has laid the groundwork for you. It is possible you are just getting started.

If uncertain, it can help to ask yourself *what would I wish for a child?*

I wonder
if
the
night sky
would hold
the same
magic
if
there
were only

one
star

I wonder who wrote the first song with C, D, and G.

I wonder if they know what they started when they did.

That neighbor next door, the one who doesn't
say too much, likely knows a thing or two.

It often seems what people most want is to be received. This comes up for me a lot when I am with someone, *receive what you are given.*

song suggestion: *Lullaby for Little Spoon*, Pete Kuzma, starting around 2:25 mark

I wonder how things might shift if each time someone were belittled they were instead belifted.

It can help to remind ourselves: people are complicated. A lot goes into making someone who they are.

someone
a lot of
something worth
making someone else
completed

R e P E
a O
E P

It often seems when we allow someone to be ordinary is when we suddenly see them as extraordinary. To be ordinary in the most extra of ways.

Honest to goodness, there've been a few times I've met someone and thought *this person is an angel.*

A stranger can do something so kind as to confound.

Some people, you meet them, and within a moment think of them as a *force*. I wonder what that is.

There are those people who – it's not just that they bring people joy. It's that people experience joy through them. What a gift, to be able to transmute joy.

If we think about it, if we really think about it, a heartbeat is the most incredible thing.

song suggestion: *winter*, MOMO

17

Re: the uncertainty principle: it may have to do with the energy of the observer. That could be why some people feel so good to be around.

I try to be mindful before I say I believe anything one way or the other.

I believe humanity is beauty in motion.

I often think of life like a spiral. It can sometimes feel you're going in circles, but you're actually moving forward.

It can help to look at your life like a timeline. Right now, today, this week and month and year, maybe couple of years, if you put it on a timeline, it's not as big.

Sometimes, you just need to rest a bit.

There may be a difference between seeking and having our eyes open. It may be that with one we are always somewhere other than where we are.

song suggestion: *It Is What It Is*, Blood Orange

It seems there is a time to step away and go within, and then there comes a time to step in and expand out.

Looking at the night sky is often a good idea.

I like how the word stellar takes something and places it among the stars.

The cosmos is huge. There is plenty of space for you to shine.

Re: the universe: it might not make much sense,
but somehow we're always being held.

Humanity, in no small part

a young boy is scared

a woman tries to get it right

He never wants people to know how scared he is. Just in general. He's really scared. Not of monsters or bullies. Just scared.

He has two younger sisters and they never seem scared. He sometimes wonders if they're scared deep down but just pretend not to be like he does, but he's pretty sure they're not scared. Just in general. They're not really all that scared.

He knows older brothers are supposed to kind of hate their younger sisters, or whatever, but he loves his like crazy. He thinks they're so cute and funny and defends them on the playground if anyone says anything mean and gives them part of his ice cream if theirs' run out first and dances with them whenever they ask him to turn on his music. If there's a thunderstorm, they both run into his room and climb into his bed and drape themselves all over and around him with the youngest, Mattie, cramming her knees into his back and the older one, Nell, spreading out over three quarters of the bed. He loves it. He likes feeling tough and strong and protective and being the person they feel safe with. He knows he's a really good brother.

It's not something that his parents taught him. He was four when Nell was born, and he remembers them saying something like 'be nice,' but they didn't have to. When they told him he was going to be a big brother and have a little sister, he was so excited. He immediately began to make drawings to decorate her room, to pick out his favorite t-shirts and pajamas to show her, to peel off some of the glow-in-the-dark star stickers from his ceiling and tape them onto the ceiling of her room, to figure out ways that he could include her in the games he made up and played by himself like *flashlight superkid* and *pajama pillow man*, and to recite some of his favorite stories about his life so far that he could tell her. He wanted to be there when she came out of his mom's stomach but his parents said maybe next time.

Same with when Mattie was born two years later. Same excitement, same preparations but with more current games, and NEW glow-in-the-dark stars because he begged his parents and they said yes and got him three of the EXACT SAME sets of stars which he put on each of their ceilings in the same way so that they were all looking at the same sky. For his birthday a few months later, he followed suit by only asking for bubble gum, root beer flavored saltwater taffy like the kind he had when he went to the beach with his grandparents, flannel pajamas, and THREE SETS OF GLOW-IN-THE-DARK PLANETS. He wrote it in all capitals to make sure his parents knew what was most important. It worked, he got the planets, and he added them to their individual starscapes.

He doesn't remember when he started to get scared. It seems like maybe he was about seven. He woke up from a bad dream sweating and with his heart racing. He tried counting the stars on his ceiling to calm himself down, but his heart kept zooming ahead. He got out of bed and went to his parents' room. He walked over to his Dad's side of the bed and tapped him on the shoulder. His dad weighed like a million pounds and didn't feel it, so he pushed on his shoulder a little harder. His dad groggily opened his eyes.

Hey, honey- everything okay?

I can't sleep. I had a bad dream.

What happened?

I can't remember.

That's okay. Do you want to get in bed with your mom and me?

Will you come to my room instead and stay until I fall back asleep?

Sure thing.

His dad fumbled around on the nightstand until he found his thick glasses, the ones he only wore at home when he took his contacts out. He took his son by the hand and walked with him down the hallway back to his room. They both climbed into the narrow twin bed.

Do you want to talk about anything?

No. I just want to fall back asleep.

Okay. Well, we can talk if you change your mind. It's okay to have bad dreams. They happen sometimes. You can always come and get your mom and me if you have one and get scared.

I'm okay. Just couldn't get back to sleep is all.

He rolled facing his dad and closed his eyes. His dad put his arm around his shoulder and squeezed just a little bit.

You're a good kid, Jack. Your mom and I know how lucky we are to have you.

Jack hid his smile and snuggled in a little closer to his dad's side.

He went to his parents' room a few more times that year when the bad dreams happened, but after a while he got embarrassed and stopped going. He felt like by this point, since he knew they were just dreams and that he was okay, that he should be able to fall back asleep by himself. But he never did. He would usually just lay there and toss around, maybe play a few games by himself, but he almost never fell back asleep. And it seems like that was about the time that he started to be scared a lot in general. Just plain scared.

Sometimes he gets so scared that he shakes. His hands especially. He sits on them to try to make them stop and it occasionally helps, but usually they're still shaking under his legs. His teacher noticed once. Ms. Ryan.

Is everything alright, Jack?

Yep.

I noticed that your hands are shaking. Did you hurt yourself?

Nope.

Do they do that a lot?

Not so much. Maybe I'm a little cold.

Okay. Well, I hope you know you can tell me if anything's on your mind.

Yep.

She hasn't asked him about it since then, but he feels like she maybe keeps an extra eye on him from time to time. He doesn't mind so much. He's often scared, so having an extra adult keep an extra eye on him from time to time is kind of nice. Especially because his parents and sisters don't know how scared he gets. It isn't so bad to have someone know. Also, Ms. Ryan is really pretty. But he DEFINITELY does not tell anyone that.

It's not like he walks around at a level ten scared all the time. It's more like it's always there. Like he'll be hanging out with his friends, or at baseball practice, or watching a movie on the couch with his sisters, or pushing the cart at the grocery store with his mom and out of nowhere he becomes terrified. His heart races, his palms sweat, his head spins. If he's standing he sometimes has to sit down. If he's sitting, he sometimes has to get up and walk around. He basically just does something, anything different from what he's already doing.

Sometimes the waves of being scared only last for a few seconds, but sometimes they last forever. Sometimes even the whole day. He just tries to stay around people on those days, hanging out with his sisters even more than usual or futzing around the kitchen when his parents are home. At this point, he's just gotten used to it being a part of who he is. And he really likes himself for the most part. It's just this whole scared thing that he can't sort out.

And for some reason, just this past week, he thought for the first time that he might ask Ms. Ryan a thing or two about it. Not directly, not talking about himself. But more just like *Hey, Ms. Ryan, math was really good today. I feel like I really learned a lot today, more than usual. I also wanted to ask you something else I was thinking about. I wonder if sometimes some people out there just kind of get scared a lot for no real reason. Just kind of suddenly get scared and they don't know why. I was wondering your thoughts on that.* He's still working on the wording and feels like he's getting pretty close. He doesn't want to lie, so he's also waiting for a day when it is an especially good math lesson.

*

[woman, *therapist*]

I hate my life.

Okay.

I don't mean that I want to kill myself.   I just hate my life.

I understand what you mean.

I think I know why.

Okay.   Why do you think that you hate your life?

I think I put all this emphasis on trying to create a life that is 'right.'   Like I'm always trying to do the right thing.   Literally.   Every single thing I do, every choice I make, every single little itty bitty thing that I ever do in any possible way, I think, 'is this right?   Is this kind and good and what's best for all of humankind?'   And when I feel like I don't do what's right, even worse if I don't do what's right *on purpose*, or with awareness, if you will, I hate myself for it, and when I do do what's right, I'm like an

43

automaton. And either way, it sucks and at the end of the day, at the end of everyday, what is actually happening is that I am not living life. I'm just thinking about it, or trying to control it, or whatever.

[It's quiet.]

I'd like to know what you think about that.

I could see how putting so much energy into always trying to do the right thing would leave someone exhausted.

I am exhausted. I also smoke and eat sugar and spike and crash all day long.

It doesn't sound like that helps much. There are times when we need to be more vigilant with ourselves than others.

No, it doesn't help. But I'm tired of hating myself for it.

I don't want you to hate yourself for it, either.

[It's quiet again.]

So then what could be some alternatives? What could be some alternatives to what you've been doing up to this point, always trying to do everything right but hating your life?

I mean, I could just be like who gives and do whatever I want. But I don't think I can do that. I mean I don't even think I'm capable of it, and even if I were, I think I would hate myself for that, too, because I do care about how my actions affect other people and I don't want to exist as a crap person in the world. I want to contribute. Like, be something good that exists on the planet in terms of the positive evolution of the human species.

Are there other alternatives you can think of?

[She thinks.]

No.

[It's quiet.]

There might be.

[It's quiet.]

I can't think of anything. And if you know them, just tell me. I know things stick better, or whatever, if they come from within or if I discover them on my own but just tell me.

There may be a way to trust that what you're doing is okay. It might have to do with trust.

I don't believe in God.

Okay. I'm not talking about religion.

Just trust in general?

Sure.

Like, the universe?

Some people put their trust in the universe. Does that speak to you?

Sometimes. But that usually just means days when I'm sitting by myself at home putting trust in the universe and not doing anything with my life.

So then what else could you trust?

[It's quiet.]

Please just tell me what you're thinking. I think about myself all day long and it's grown old and feels like it's passed awareness and teetering on narcissim and it's nice to hear someone else's thoughts.

[The therapist smiles.]

You're not a narcissist. I know narcissists. You're not one.

I'm getting close.

You've got a ways to go.

[They laugh a little. It gets quiet again.]

What if you trusted yourself?

[This is hard for the woman to hear.]

I've lost a lot of trust in myself. I'm not sure I can do that.

I've gained a lot of trust in you.

[The woman becomes emotional.]

Thank you.

You're welcome.

I'm scared.

I know.

I don't want to feel like I'm wasting my life. Or my *brain*. My *mind*. My heart. I'm so closed off. My heart is awesome. I have so much to give to the world.

I know you do. You will.

I don't want to get dementia from loneliness or sugar or lack of sleep. Those are three big aspects of my life.

I don't want you to get dementia either.

[It's quiet.]

I hope you know how much you mean to me.

I do.

I don't mean to be inappropriate. I'm just grateful you are in my life.

I know you are. I'm grateful for you in my life, too.

[As if the therapist knows what she's thinking-]

I didn't have to say that. It's not against the rules for us to care about our patients and be affected by them. But I do think you actually believe me. These things take time.

I know they do. But I feel like I'm running out of time. Or that I'm already out of time and in denial about seeing it.

[It's quiet, save for the crying.]

I'm so scared.

[She sees the clock. It's over time.]

Sorry.

[She pulls herself together.   She gets out her checkbook.]

Next time.

Please.

I'm further along down this road than you are.

*

53

big sur, he beckoned me;
but it was ojai, she spoke to me.
she said *my love, you're here to see;*
let me hold you, so you can breathe.

at any given moment, I'd like to walk barefoot
on a bed of moss in a bed of ferns by the bed of a
creek.

it is interesting to me what stays around longest.
turtles and trees come to mind. it seems they
may know a thing or two about how to live well.

sometimes our bodies and souls move at
different speeds. we may still be growing into
ourselves.

tears release beauty

    j u s t

t h i n k

     o f

  w i n t e r

    w h e n

  i t

s   n   o   w   s

song suggestion: *Hush,* Tourist

a dream in three parts: part one

I had a dream last night
a young woman,
or was it a girl,
I believe
a young woman
held up a picture,
a drawing,
of an elephant.
the elephant was in profile
moving from left to right.
it seems there were
a few adornments
around it's head
giving it
a regal feel.

If there is a spot nearby, a roof or a building or a
hill, it may be worth going to the top every so
often and taking a look out.

An interesting visual: someone wearing an eye
mask standing next to someone using binoculars.

Instead of knocking others down to build
ourselves up, let's just build each other up.

Some wounds may just take a little longer to heal.

It can be easy to accidentally forget all the times
in your life when you were really brave.

song suggestion: *Bloodflow*, Grandbrothers

I like the breakdown of the word compassion.

with or *together* plus *strong and barely controllable emotion* or *an intense desire or enthusiasm for something.*

I suppose an additional definition for compassion can then be *with a barely controllable emotion of intense desire and enthusiasm for togetherness.*

References:

passion: https://en.oxforddictionaries.com/definition/passion
co,com: https://www.learnthat.org/pages/view/roots.html#c

Just think about it: if everyone changes one
person's life for the better, the whole world is
better off.

$1 + 1 = 7,600,000,000$

It can sometimes seem like we don't have each other's back, but we do.

It is possible to hold space for two things at once. For two opposites to exist simultaneously. It can help to think of it visually by holding both of your hands out in front of you, palms up.

Sometimes I dress tough and sometimes I dress soft. Both feel good.

You and me, we all have our flaws. At some point, it seems we choose which ones we are okay with and which ones we are not okay with. And then, we choose if we do something about it.

Go for it.

song suggestion: *Fading Nights (feat. Anna Naklab)*, Parra for Cuva

I hope that I treat people well. That I am kind, that I am honest, and that I am generous. And when I am not, that I more readily notice it and then do something about it.

Something I have come to ask myself is if I am
doing something out of fear or in spite of fear. I
do my best to follow the latter.

If you know little of Athena, perhaps a moment
to look her up.

It seems a lot of wisdom lies somewhere in the navigation between building confidence and gaining humility. It can be unclear which is which, but I trust that I am learning.

I've always loved how there are so many
different ways in which people are smart.
Athletes seeing and thinking and moving
spatially, as if they see the court or the field or
the ice and the arrangements of the other
players and the potential movements of the
other bodies through space as they move into
that space and both operate within and actively
shift its configuration. Mathematicians seeing
and thinking and moving numbers and patters,
bringing numbers and patterns to life and
applying them to nearly everything that
surrounds them, writers conveying the
innermost essence of a fictitious character and
somehow enabling a stranger reading it to meet
the character or live vicariously through the
character or heal in their relation to the
character, musicians who hear and see the world
in music, channeling it through their instrument
and conveying something never before
experienced by anyone until the musician brings
it to life, painters and sculptors and architects
and designers and builders who likewise create
in reality what formerly existed only in their
minds and of which even they may not have
fully seen in their minds eye but brought to
fruition through the process of how their mind

works, people with such profound emotional intelligence they can be among nearly anyone and somehow be able to relate to them and to empathize with them and to understand them at a core level. How would schools ever be able to assess one's intelligence or abilities when the ways in which people are intelligent and able are both infinite and incomparable? Teachers are incredible.

I like the word majestic. It takes something and
exalts it in one fell swoop.

Have you ever watched someone do what they do and thought *I'm watching greatness right now*. It's amazing how you kind of know it every time, almost the moment it kicks in.

Deft hands mesmerize me. I could watch a locksmith for hours. Same with a potter. I would have liked to see Michelangelo at work.

This one friend, when she talks about something she's passionate about, it's like I get to watch her mind spark thought into being. She astonishes me.

Different responses of different people to different music interests me. How some respond so strongly to some music and others so strongly to some other music. I think of this as some people being tuned into some frequencies and other people being tuned into other frequencies. It seems I can nearly tell in an instant if someone and I are tuned into the same frequency. And I can definitely tell if I see them dance.

song suggestion: *Coming Back Around*, NEIL FRANCES

It always seems a good to get a little weird
sometimes. Just a touch.

song suggestion: *Neutron* Dance, Krystal Klear

I'm bringing *I got a beef with you* back.

Anyone who doesn't like lush forests, I got a beef with you.

Humanity, in no small part

a barista uses a ladder

a tree becomes a desk

Dear Stranger Barista,

My hunch is that you are a really smart person.
I can just tell.

You are pretty and have an unassuming, non-
invasive voice, and I hope you are valued for
that and not taken advantage of for it. I am
speaking about by those in your private life. I
hope that if you find yourself in a relationship
that it is one of love, and that your significant
other recognizes how lucky he/she is to be
around a gentle soul, and to not presume that a
gentle soul equates with lack of intelligence
because, as previously said, I am thinking you
are a really smart person.

My hot chocolate is excellent. You made it
exactly as I ordered it, and I thank you for that.
It was also exorbitant, but that is on me. Were
you surprised that I ordered a hot chocolate?
People sometimes are.

I wonder which part of New York you live in.
Probably Brooklyn, as most people your age (I'm
presuming early twenties) live in Brooklyn,

although it is equally possible that you live in Washington Heights or Queens. Maybe Harlem. You could also live around the corner.

I think you did well in Math in high school, but your art is what makes you stand out. It is where you find your voice. It surprises people. It is what makes people want to get to know you better. I think people should want to get to know you anyway, but I am guessing they really want to get to know you when they see you as you are, which most readily comes through in your art. That is when you shift in their eyes.

Somehow you made a blue button-down oxford and black skinny jeans look cool and unique. I think it is your long side braid. Don't worry. I am not attracted to you. Can you tell? A small part of me hates myself every time I wonder if someone wonders about my sexuality. This is something I would like to change about myself. Caring what others think, and hating myself every time I care. We all have our things we're working on.

I fear there may be a very deep sadness in you. It can come with the artistic energy from time to time. I hope you are able to channel it into your work with relative ease. To give it somewhere to live so that it merely passes through you and does not consume you. This is something that can take time to learn how to do. I hope you are hanging in there.

I hope you have a network of friends here. I am thinking you have a lot of girl friends, and probably not too many guy friends. As I write this, however, I realize that I could be way off. If someone told me that most of your friends were guys, I would believe them. If that is the case, I think a lot of them would have crushes on you. And if not a lot, then that one guy. Your closest friend. He's been in love with you for years. Sometimes you think you might love him and want to be with him. There was that one time, those two times you accidentally hooked up – the first time when you were sad after that bad breakup, and the second time after that party that night. You've wondered if you love him, but you know deep down that you do not. It's his love for you that you feel, which is what makes you wonder. But you know that you would walk all over him. It's hard for you to let him go, though. You need his love too much.

You think you should feel guiltier about this than you do, but you rarely feel guilty. You like to get what you want. I cannot tell how I feel about this aspect of you.

Part of what made you seem smart to me was how you went about getting the container of almond milk down from the shelf. You took the extra moment to set up the stepladder. A lot of people would have tried to finagle it down and in the process either knocked things over, dropped the milk, hurt their arm, or taken three times as long as it would have taken to just set up the ladder. I also liked that because I was your first customer and you had just opened, you asked me to wait a moment so that you could wipe down my table before I sat down. You did not have to do that because I would not have known the difference. Thank you. Maybe you do not treat your guy friend that way. Maybe you try to be honest with him, and you only want what's best for him. I could have been wrong. I am sorry.

Because you are working the morning shift, I hope and trust that you have fun plans for yourself tonight. There is a full moon rising, though I doubt those types of things affect you much. You seem pretty grounded to the earth.

I hope you receive good tips today. I trust the table-wiping and stepladder mentality will contribute to that happening.

Best regards,

Man seated at the small round table in back

*

He walked into his office and closed the door. Something about closing the door allowed him to shut out the world behind him. It did not work perfectly. He could still hear voices, he could still feel the ground shake slightly whenever someone passed by, when someone pushed their chair across the floor, the wheels occasionally catching on the cheap gray carpet's knots, when someone dropped their bag onto the floor, when a delivery man dropped a heavy box at someone's cubicle. They existed, but they existed less with the door shut.

He sat down at his desk. His great-grandfather's desk. The one made from the wood from the trees taken down at the family farm so many years ago. Probably a hundred years ago by now. *That tree would be over a hundred years old by now*, he thought. *Instead, this desk is over a hundred years old*. Something about this felt wrong to him. But sitting at his great-grandfather's desk felt right. He never met his great-grandfather. David Lloyd Strong. What a name. It was his maternal great-grandfather. He would give anything to have the last name Strong. Instead, his last name was Bixson. He was fine with Bixson.

He opened up his laptop and glanced at his calendar. A few afternoon meetings, a conference call at four. He had promised Caroline he would pick up Mary from her soccer practice at 4:30. He would have to call Caroline and tell her about the conference call. She would understand. She always understood. She should leave him. He had thought it a million times. If he loved her the way she deserved, he would insist that she leave him. Instead, he loved her because he desperately needed her in his life, and as such, he was always grateful. *I'm a selfish man. I always have been.*

There was a knock at the door.

"Come in."

It was Marshall. Marshall was a relatively new employee, a part of the team only six months or so. He was hard-working and eager, and he mainly kept to himself unless otherwise necessary.

"The manufacturer called. They said they tried everything they could, but they won't be able to get it out until first thing in the morning. What would you like me to tell Cameron?"

Cameron was the head of their biggest client, Grove Paper Company, and he was difficult and demanding, as well as thorough, loyal, and dependable. He hated to let Cameron down.

"I'll give him a call. Thank you."

"Shall I close the door behind me?"

"Yes, thank you."

The door was again closed. It wasn't the same as having shut it himself, but it still helped.

He closed the browser for his calendar and opened his music files. He scrolled until he landed on *Daily Practices, Meditation Series, Part 2*. He further scrolled until he landed on *Day 11*. He put on his headphones. Soft music began, the soft music then joined by raindrops. He undid the top two buttons of his shirt, relaxed into his chair, and closed his eyes. He was sure he was doing this wrong. He was always sure he was doing it wrong. But he never cared. He thought about whatever he wanted to think about. He closed his eyes if he felt like it. He just liked the music, and he liked the raindrops.

He wasn't that relaxed. His chest still hurt. He was still preoccupied by his constipation. He still had not called Caroline or Cameron. But he still just liked the raindrops.

Several minutes passed. The music and raindrops faded. More light music began. A gentle clap of thunder. He glanced at his monitor. *Lesson 12*. No harm, no foul. He liked gentle thunder, as well.

*

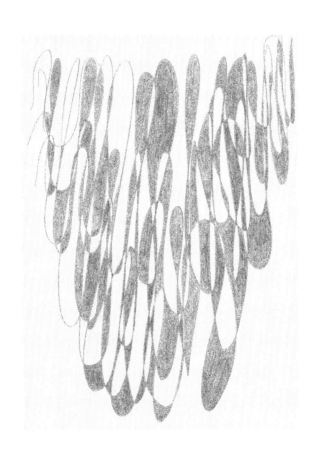

103

I once met a redwood tree
she told me her children had died
I asked her how I could help
she said *you can stand by my side*

I spoke to a dove one day
    she landed on my window sill
        and later, she flew away

when I was six, I dreamt I was riding a white
horse underwater. we were in the ocean, and we
rode in large circles, free of harness and reins,
the water illuminated from above, both of us
able to breathe freely. as an adult, I have
wondered if the horse's name may have been
spirit.

I sometimes think of it this way: nature is what's inside, and nurture is everything else, which is a lot.

and sometimes this way: nature is one's essence, nurture is creating the space for them to shine.

and also: nature is what comprises us, nurture is who holds us.

and: nature is who they are, nurture is allowing them to be.

song suggestion: *Pensiero Stupendo − Original Mix*, Róisín Murphy

if you're ever in a place where there are herons,
watch them until they take flight. that's the best
part.

picturing a feather can help with some things.

I've grown to see life as a spectrum. In speaking to grief, I hold my hands a foot or so apart and say *life used to be like this*. I then hold my hands as far apart as they can go and say *and now it's like this*. The spectrum of life expands. One becomes aware of the pains, sorrows, and heartaches not yet before known, as well as the beauties, joys, and lights not yet before seen. One is broken open and, in breaking open, extends in every direction. One becomes flooded with the beauty of what it means to be alive.

It seems we could presume as to the level of someone's pain or as to the ability of their resiliency, or we could hold space for someone's pain and honor their resiliency.

As painful as some moments may be, it can be helpful to remember that some moments heal all pain.

It's all in the definition.

humanity:

1. all human beings collectively; the human race;
   humankind

2. the quality or condition of being human; human nature

3. the quality of being humane; kindness; benevolence

Reference:

www.dictionary.com/browse/humanity?s=t

One of my greatest wishes for people is self-love
and self-respect. A lot of healing seems to occur
when those things first come to pass. It may
have to do with self-worth.

Though the bad decisions matter, the good ones
matter so much more.

If your soul is feeling lonely, perhaps try putting your left hand on your heart and your right hand on your stomach. This can help open up direct communication between the beat of your life and the base of your being, and they say two minds think better than one.

We hear a lot about finding one's other half, but two wholes sounds like a whole lot more.

Home is where we feel safe, seen, held and free.
It has been said it resides within.

The thing about New York City is that within one block, any block, one may encounter the entire spectrum of humankind. I have learned it is important for this to be a consistent part of my life.

I think of New York City as my heartbeat and the Pacific Northwest as my soul. My home resides amongst, in between and on either side.

These are my plants: monstera, bird of paradise, jade, aloe.

These are my people: redwoods.

I've always found quite beautiful the countless iterations of what constitutes a family.

Perhaps we will one day elect a queen who acts on behalf of the people of the world.

It seems the world is teeming with people fired up to do great things.

It's good to have some fire in the belly. Fire it up.

song suggestion: *The Fire*, The Roots, John Legend

Sometimes laughing feels like it comes from a place deep in the stomach that knows no bottom. Like no matter how hard you laugh, you can't reach the source of the feeling.

Isn't rhythm incredible? It can go away, we keep it somewhere, and when it comes back, we're still with it.

The bottom half of my body keeps the bassline while the top half plays the melody. So far as I can tell, it's out of my hands.

I think even the Beatles might agree that some songs may be better off without that bridge.

Do what you do.

Music and dance are amazing in their ability to release energy, transforming it from stagnancy into beauty. They help turn that which may harm into that which heals.

The world is on the cusp of a dance revolution.
I'll help lead it if you'll join me.

[shake, shake, deal]

song suggestion: *Otic*, Alex Metric, Ten Ven

Own your power. It's incredible how much you have.

Whoever invented music, when did the other person first join in?

Whoever invented dancing, how did you know when it became more than what it was the moment before?

Whoever invented magic, was the pleasure in the achievement of disbelief or the belief of the achievement? How did you know the difference?

Whoever invented the word love, how did you know it when you got it right?

Words carry a lot of weight. They give voice to our being.

When I love, I love fiercely.

138

A child's laughter? Really, it's everything.

If it's the choice that most heals, I'd say it's a go.
Most others, I'd say it's a pause.

If it's to protect a child, it's a go.

It is possible both to see the child within another and to hold adults accountable for their actions. It seems this may be one of the greatest beauties of humanity.

They say it's all about love. The thing is, seems
as though they're right.

I am choosing to believe that if this reaches
someone and is of some help to them in some
way then it is worthwhile.

*

Sometimes, when I think about what we know, what we've discovered and learned, and what we don't know, the possibilities, outer space and everything in it, dark matter and dark energy, I imagine looking at the Earth from far away in space when we've launched a rocket or a spaceship. What that looks like on Earth. The launch, the rumble and blare and firing of the engines, the power and force and tumult experienced by the astronauts inside during the launch, the effort of the machine to rise. And then what it looks like from far away in space. A small blue and green dot far away, and this smaller little white and gray speck that bops up, maybe loops around a bit, then bops back down.

If I were to draw it, I would take a piece of paper, put a small circle in the corner, and then put a little dot outside of that circle with a line indicating that the dot bopped up, then bopped back down.

song suggestion: *Our Corner of the Universe*, K.S. Rhoads

Humanity, in no small part

a man walks into a bar

A man walks into a bar. The bartender asks him what it will be. He says it will be bourbon. He does not think about it before he says it. If he had, he may have ordered something else. A cosmopolitan. Not because it is his favorite drink, but because he has always wanted to try one. And trying one among strangers would have been an ideal situation. He is a man's man, after all.

The bartender begins to make his drink. The man sits up a bit, something he often reminds himself to do. He has a tendency to slump, and they say improving your posture can improve your mood. But he's so tired, and the slump feels better, so he settles back into comfort.

The bartender places his drink before him. He's glad the bartender made it neat, as he forgot to specify. Does it show that he's the kind of guy who prefers it neat? He glances at the man sitting to his left. The man wears business pants and a dress shirt, two buttons undone at the top. He likely wore a coat and tie earlier, but they did not make their way into the bar. The man to his left looks down at his drink, a brown drink over ice. Judging by the melted ice cubes and damp napkin surrounding the glass, he's been holding it for a while. *Probably not an alcoholic. What a strange thing to think*, as if he may have otherwise presumed the man an alcoholic.

He takes a quick look around for peanuts or some such bar food. A sad bowl of popcorn sits in an old small brown bowl a few seats down. Sad though it is, he wants some. He looks in the direction long enough that the man sitting before the popcorn looks up as one often does when one senses someone looking at them. The man gives a slight nod towards the popcorn, as if to say *is that free?* The other man nudges the bowl down the bar. The man pulls it the rest of the way.

He takes a small handful and pours it into his mouth. It's salty and a little chewy, exactly as he suspected. He washes it down with a sip of the bourbon. He realizes this is his first sip and wonders if anyone has watched him as he briefly watched the man to his left. For if they had, they would likely surmise that he, too, is not an alcoholic given how long it took him to have his first sip.

Without asking, the bartender tears open a large plastic bag of popcorn and adds some to the bowl. The new additions are a slightly different color than the existing few, more orange and yellow though clearly from the same brand. He nods a thank you even though he is a little sad, as he knows the new kernels will not be as chewy- a personal preference, albeit an odd one.

He takes another sip of his drink, an intentionally smaller sip. He likes to savor his drinks. He likes to savor. It is one of life's few small perks that we can control. Savoring, that is.

He tries not to think about his day. Not because anything particularly bad happened, but because he is working on being more present in his life. He knows that being present allows one to enjoy the journey as it happens, as life happens. And so he continues to read books on the journey and the moment and to not think about the past when he does things like have a neat bourbon in a bar with a bowl of both chewy and fresh-from-the-bag popcorn.

153

He becomes aware of the TV playing in the upper right-hand corner of the room. Some sort of sports highlight show replays home runs and near-home runs that were miraculously caught. Baseball. He makes a small harrumph. He enjoys a good night out with the guys, but the sport always makes him chuckle just a little bit.

He reaches into his pants pocket and pulls out his phone. He clicks it to life, not because he's expecting any texts or e-mails, but because this is what people so often do when sitting by themselves so as to appear to be doing something. To seem like they are expecting something. On most occasions, he would scan through old conversations, old correspondences, unanswered requests, but tonight he returns his phone to his pocket. A small victory, though in what, he cannot say.

The bartender runs the rag in front of him as he wipes the counter. He throws the rag over his shoulder and sets to making another drink. The man watches him work, pouring drinks and scooping ice and placing straws, unconscious yet attentive in his repetitive and ever-changing routine. *There is something about flow and process in his work*, he muses. *I wonder if he is aware of that. I wonder if he were if it would change.*

He takes a second sip of his drink, again proudly noting his cool pace. And yet again, he is reminded of the man to his left, who likewise continues to hold his beaded glass and its melted contents of diluted brown company. His first impression having been so positive, the man's glass now makes him very, very sad.

And then, all at once, as if struck by an epiphany, he realizes that this is the worst day of his life. There have been bad days, days when he felt more melancholy than others, days when he had a hard time getting out of bed. But this is different. This is very, very different. Never before has he thought *this is the worst day of my life.*

It is made all the worse by the fact that he is aware of it as it is happening. He is entirely conscious of everything he is feeling, of the cloak upon his back, of the weights in his shoes, of the soul seeping its way out of his body, more gone now than when he first entered the bar.

Can the others tell? Is it so obvious? It must be. No posture or acknowledgment of the process or slow sips of his drink will mask that today is the very worst day of his life.

He is scared. He is scared of what this means. He is scared because he fears he does not have the tools to handle such sadness, such truth, such life. *They do not teach us this,* he thinks. They do not teach one how to turn the worst day of one's life into something else. They do not teach us how to be reminded of the many things that make all of the other days not the worst days of our lives. They do not teach us what to do with the worst day of one's life as it is happening versus something seen in retrospect. Whoever they are, whoever we allude to when we say they do or do not teach us these sorts of things, they definitely do not teach us this.

He does not know where to look. He does not know what to do. With his hands, with his feet, if he should cross his legs or place both on the barstool's footrest. Should he pull out his phone, muster the energy to look through old texts and e-mails and websites to seem occupied, to seem like someone experiencing an average day in his life?

His breath gets short. He has a hard time pulling in full ones. He tugs at the front of his shirt so as to create a little more space for his lungs to expand and recede. He shifts the waist of his pants, adjusts his collar. Reflexively, he puts his glass against his forehead. The cold and damp feel good for a brief moment before he quickly lowers it for fear that he call any attention to himself.

Can they tell? They must.

He looks again at the man to his left. Though this time, an entirely different feeling overwhelms him. Not one of admiration, nor one of sadness, but one of pure and utter envy. For surely the chances of two men sitting next to each other experiencing what is becoming the unbearably worst days of their lives are naught. And so, he becomes racked with envy to have whatever day that man is having. Any day other than his own. Other than this moment. Because this is unbearable.

157

And yet he must. He must bear it. Because he does not want to die.

Confusion sets in. He takes a sip.

I do not want to die.

I do not want to die.

I do not want to die.

To embark on not dying becomes his focus. And in order to do this, he becomes acutely aware that he needs to breathe his soul back to life, his soul now hanging by the last thread of its being. As if some outer force is pulling it from his core, the roots of its webbing just barely keeping their grip. *I need to save my soul. I need to reel my soul back into my being.*

He takes a sip of his drink. A few moments later, he takes another. He has a few handfuls of the popcorn. He tries to focus on his chewing, on the taste of the salt as it mixes with the aftermath of the bourbon.

A woman walks in and sits down at the opposite end of the bar. She is likely in her mid-forties, and she dresses appropriately for her age. What that means, he is not sure, but the phrase came to him as he made a passing judgment of her character and life. She did well in high school, was a well-liked and respectable teammate in some sport like soccer or lacrosse, though not the star, she was above-average pretty with a stream of healthy relationships throughout college and her twenties, and she now has a successful career in which she is both well-liked and well-respected. Her personal life after twenty-eight or so becomes murky to him. If he saw her in the grocery store, he would think *a lawyer, married to a man four years her senior with two kids, a three-year age difference between the older son and the younger daughter, able to win a trial in the morning and arrive in time for the first pitch at her son's baseball game and the opening number at her daughter's dance recital.* That would make perfect sense, he thought, but she is here, in this bar, and so it does not. In fact, nothing about her makes sense. Unless she is in town for work, in which case everything would make sense again. He overhears her order a glass of Sauvignon Blanc. She takes a handful of popcorn while she waits. Having either suddenly forgotten or just remembered something, she pulls out her phone and busily taps at its screen. He watches her fingers move. It could be one of a million things. She forgot to ask how her daughter's test went, to tell her husband she arrived safely, to send the file to the demanding client, to finish her game of solitaire. His breathing continuing its increasing pace, he turns his attention back from this game of what-ifs and fantasies to his drink, leaving the woman with her real life behind him and willing himself not to think *a woman like that would never love a man like me*.

A woman like that would never love a man like me.

A woman like that would never love a man like me.

Each breath continues to grow more shallow, one after the other somehow lodging itself just below his Adam's apple before the next one comes in. He locks his gaze on the glass cradled between his two hands, thankful for a singular point of focus as he counts his inhalations and exhalations. *One, two, three, four. Pause. Four, three, two, one. Pause. One, two, three, four. Pause. A woman like that would never love a man like me. Pause.*

The bartender places the newly filled bowl before him.

"Can I get you a refill on your drink?"

"Sure, thank you."

And just like that, it is better. He feels better. That small interaction is all it took to make everything better. To make his entire life better. This has happened in the past. When he saw no way out from the breathing, from the gasping, from the assurance that the next breath might be his last, and then something so seemingly small occurs that distracts him for the briefest moment of time after which everything is gone. A lifetime of fear and pain erased. All of it. Does the bartender, like the others before him, know what he just did for him? Does the bartender know that he just saved his life? The obvious answer should be no, but a part of the man thinks *maybe he does. Maybe the bartender does know what he just did, and maybe he has done it a thousand times before for a thousand different people not all that different from myself.* The thought simultaneously shames and comforts the man.

As might be expected, he finds himself suddenly feeling much closer to the bartender. Like they share a bond, perhaps a bond like that of soldiers who have been through an experience together that would be impossible to describe in full to someone who had not been through it. That singular sort of shared experience that will forever connect two people together. Although the bartender may be somewhat aware of his heroism, the man concedes to himself that the bartender does not likewise feel this bond. Because even if the bartender knows what he just participated in, he has participated in it a thousand times before with a thousand different people and, as such, only feels one one-thousandth of the connection that the man feels. The man allows for this discrepancy in connection, and he trusts that by the end of the evening, he will likewise allow the bartender to return to earth as the humble mortal he in fact is.

He wills himself not to look in the direction of the woman sitting at the end of the bar. This is a skill he has learned to hone the last several years, to not torment himself further than is necessary. He sometimes wonders if this system works because there is something to be said for the actual tormenting itself creating a sense of closeness or meaning. But he chooses to rise above that, as he sees it, and as a result neither torments himself nor has meaning. *Surely there is a level in between*, he occasionally permits himself, though more frequently, he succumbs to the potential reality that there is not. That one either lives fully amidst the possibility of many tortures, or one secludes oneself from potential torture and instead lives in solitude, devoid of meaning or connection.

A man sits down in the seat to his left. He did not realize how territorial he had become about his space until it was intruded. It makes perfect sense that this intruder would choose the seat he chose, as there are few vacant seats at the bar, and even fewer with empty seats next to them. Reflexively, he scoots his stool ever so slightly to the right, somehow reclaiming some of his space by creating a new circumference of which he is the center. The intruder takes a handful of popcorn from what was his bowl. Protective, he finds some small solace in knowing that the man will not get any of the slightly chewy pieces, as he got the majority of those to himself before the bartender altered the popcorn constitution. He does not hate this intruder, he tells himself. He just hates that this intruder, this other man, ruined this moment of his life. This moment that moments before was the worst day of his life, followed by a moment of awareness as to the precarious situation surrounding his soul, followed by a moment of acknowledgment of a love he will never receive, followed by a moment of a profound bonding in brotherhood. He concedes that the intruder may provide a new moment of something unforgettable in his life, though he deems the chances unlikely. Much about the last hour, two hours, *how long have I been here?*, were unexpected, even in their extreme ordinariness. And with that, as if struck by a moment of beauty, he allows himself the wisp of a belief that *anything is possible. A woman like that just might love a man like me. I once fell from the top of a magnolia tree as a child. I should not have survived the fall. But I did. A woman like that may very well love a man like me. I want to go home.*

He motions to the bartender for his tab, the thought suddenly arising from deep in his being

I will be okay. I may not know how, but I believe in somehow.

The intruder takes another handful of popcorn from their bowl. The bartender places a brown drink with ice before the intruder, followed by the tab before the man. He takes a couple of twenties from his wallet and leaves them with the receipt, the asking of the tab more a formality than a necessity, as he knew the approximate cost and likewise knew that he would well exceed the amount and standard twenty-percent tip as a small token of appreciation for the bartender having earlier saved his life.

The man heads for the door. The bartender looks up from his glass-washing and nods a goodbye, which the man returns. He walks the length of the bar, passing the woman on his right. He reaches the door, stops, then turns around. He approaches the woman. He stands just behind her left shoulder. *I might have loved you, if only for a moment. Though I would have loved you fiercely.*

Aware of the gentleman hovering behind her, she turns from her phone and looks him directly in the eye.

"May I help you?"

He makes to scan the contents of the bar.

"No, excuse me, I'm sorry. I thought that I may have forgotten something. I see now that I have not. Have a good evening."

She nods a likewise and turns back to her phone. He heads back to the door and walks outside.

*

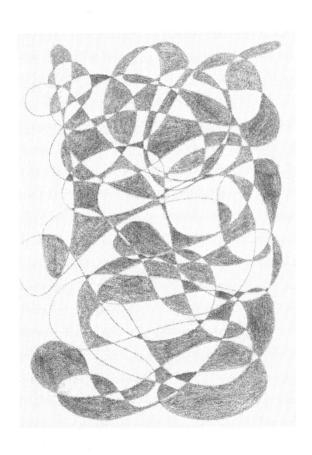

you are here, and if you are here, then you are
alive. and if you are alive, then the greatest
contribution you make to your life and, as such,
to our collective evolution is to best *live*, which
means to live comprehensively. and if you allow
for this, if you allow for both the joys and the
pains as aspects of what it means to be
comprehensively alive, you begin to transform
each moment of pain from something that
defines you into that which heals you. every
moment you heal, we heal. we're all in this
thing together.

i

p

r

o

m

i

s

e

song suggestion: *Do Not Let Your Spirit Wane*, Gang of Youths

if
you
are
broken
one
day
that
rubble
will
become
the
blocks
with
which
you
build
your
N e w F o u n d a t i o n

172

I dream in shades of jade
in colors of stone
in animal form
in mystical realms

it's worth visiting the desert.
it may surprise you.
see what happens if you go it alone.
you may surprise you.

       when   I   think   of   stillness
I   think   of   a   lake   with   not
       a   ripple   in   it.

the difference between overhead lighting and lamps is like the difference between noon and sunset.

the

word

d   p   l
  a   p   e

b r i n g s

l   g   t
  i   h

t o

l f
  i   e

177

you may question your intuition,
don't.
you may question your decisions,
don't.
hold fast to who you are.
you did everything right.
because I say so
and because you know so.

a dream in three parts: part two

it seems
she was showing it
to another woman
and me,
or maybe there were
a few of us.
I seemed to be just
slightly to the side.
she held it
in a way
almost akin
to that of an
elementary school teacher,
though not like
she was above us.
it seems
we were the older ones.

There are occasionally those moments you wish everyone could share. That everyone could experience exactly what you are experiencing exactly as you experience it. One fourth of July, I was driving home on the freeway and it happened that my drive coincided with the onset of every fireworks show in the area. And so for twenty-five miles, the freeway was lined with fireworks displays, some exploding directly over the freeway, more extending miles into the distance on either side as jubilant backdrops, supporting orchestras. It was as though the timing of the displays were perfectly synced with the timing of my route home, each display erupting into life as my car passed by, which didn't make sense. I was driving east. You'd think the displays in the east would have erupted before the displays in the west. I can most closely describe it as twenty-five minutes of magic in motion.

song suggestion: *Ancora Tu*, Róisín Murphy

Every now and again, something takes my breath away.

As a child, I often thought *there are too many coincidences for them to be coincidences.* As an adult, I often think *that doesn't mean we have to know what they are.*

It does not matter what we call it, but we can tell when we're living from it, and we can feel when we're around it.

I believe in the possibility of everything we do not know.

If something seems magical, perhaps just let it be magical.

song suggestion: *Myvatna*, by Dreyma

What do you think of when you think of the
beauty of one's soul?

I believe in the capability of each individual.

Same math, $1 + 1 = 7,600,000,000$

I would rather stand beside you than compare
myself to you.

Instead of liking it when great people are self-deprecating, I prefer to like them because they are great. It makes sense that two likes would go further than one.

Some seem driven by doing what they have to do to get what they want. I suppose I wonder if that will lead them to what they really want.

I always wanted to be someone's muse. Can't help it.

Biology aside, there is something quite beautiful about the distinction between being a girl and becoming a woman. It seems to do with going from someone who others want you to be to who you are. I imagine it's a similar distinction between being a boy and becoming a man. Or any variation in between. Ownership of self does not discriminate.

Thank goodness people are more readily using the word strength when describing femininity. It's one of the best parts.

It can sometimes help to pause, turn your head over your shoulder, and take a brief look back at where you started. You've come further than you think.

*

there is a dream in which I am riding a mat at rapid speed. similar to how one might ride a magic carpet, though only a few inches off the ground. it is night, and I fly past wherever it is I am going. my dad is around, and there is a sense of having zoomed right past him. I loop back around, and as I do, I see the mountain before me above which the starscape looms and encompasses the majority of the sky. the sky is a deep night purple and the stars infinite. the thought is *let that be enough*.

song suggestion: *Kusanagi*, ODESZA

*

Tree roots interest me. Each root different, some roots entangled, all of which emerge from and converge towards the creation of one tree that builds, holds, and sustains itself by pulling from all of these different, somehow ultimately interconnected sources. A forest's roots all but boggles my mind.

Chances are, a good handful of the strangers standing around you are fantastic.

I often wonder why compete when we can compel.

It seems who we know is less interesting than getting to know someone.

Re: giving and receiving: I am thinking the
secret to beauty lies somewhere in here, perhaps
next to the secret to joy, amid the secret to
connection, alongside the secret to humanity.

There are some people in a lot of pain. If you are not, perhaps give them a moment of beauty. If you are, perhaps let yourself receive the moment.

Just remember, we're not robots.

unless you have never made a mistake. then you are a robot.

song suggestion: *Something Human*, Muse

Humanity, in no small part

*a woman who nodded likewise at a bar once had a
question for a woman who once tried to get it right*

a heroic bartender who loves hot chocolate once met a desk

*the child of a man who walked into a bar grew to love the
one who intruded on his popcorn*

"Mom?"

"Yes, sweetheart?"

"I was just wondering what happens when we die."

The mother looked up from her newspaper.

Lucy sat on the couch, looking at her mother expectantly.

"Mom?"

"I heard you, sweetheart. It's a thoughtful question. I'm just thinking about what to say because I want to give you a thoughtful answer."

"Take your time. I'm not busy."

Lucy watched her mom as thoughtfully as she could, hoping it might help her come up with her thoughtful response.

"Well, I suppose it depends on who you ask."

"Why?"

"Well, one person might have a different opinion than another."

"Martha said that we go to heaven because that's where her grandmother went. But when she told me what heaven was, it didn't make any sense to me. I tried to think of living forever, but the more I thought about it, the more it seemed impossible. Then I tried to think about nothing happening at all when we die, but I couldn't imagine not being alive and not being able to think, either. It made my head want to burst. Martha got upset when I told her that it didn't make sense to me."

"It sounds like it makes sense to Martha that her grandmother went to heaven."

"What do you think?"

Lucy's mom folded the paper and set it aside. She went over to the couch and sat next to her daughter.

"I suppose I think there is enough space in the world for people to believe different things, so long as it does not cause anyone else harm."

"So do you believe Martha or someone else in the world?"

"I believe what they think is true for each of them, and I accept that."

Lucy made a face.

"Huh?"

Lucy's mom thought for a moment.

"Well, sometimes the way people think about what happens after we die has to do with their religion. And there are different types of religions all over the world. And the people who practice those different religions think differently about things like where we come from, all of the stuff in outer space, or what happens to us after we die. And some people aren't religious at all and have their own views on those things that make sense to them. And some people really like what science says about these things, and some other people like a mishmash of everything. A whole lot of people think a whole lot of different things about it all. That's part of what makes everyone so unique and different."

"How many different religions are there?"

"Oh gosh, hundreds? Thousands? I'm not sure."

"How do they think differently about it all? Why don't they just all think the same thing"

Lucy's mom looked down at her daughter.

"These are some pretty tough questions, sweetheart. Even for your mom."

Lucy stared ahead, neither satisfied nor dissuaded in her interest.

"Okay, well, let's see, some people think there is someone or something called a god, or sometimes several gods, who created everything. And some of those people think that the god or gods are involved in everything that goes on here on earth, and in the stars and galaxies, and even after we die, while others think that the god or gods don't get involved in those things too much. Some other people don't think of it so much as a god but as something called divinity, and that divinity exists within everybody. Sometimes it's described as a light if it helps you to think of it that way."

Lucy pictured a light inside of everybody. The thought of it made her smile.

"I like picturing people with lights. It's hard to imagine someone sad if they always have a light on inside."

Lucy picked at the hem of her shirt.

"But what about the people who aren't religious and don't believe in a god, or in a lot of gods, or in a light inside of everyone? What do they think happens when we die?"

"There are lots of people who don't believe in anything at all. They might be okay with not knowing all of the answers to everything, unlike someone I know..."

Lucy's mom playfully nudged her daughter.

"You would have to talk to each person to find out how they felt."

"Mom?"

"Yes, love?"

"But what do you think? What do you think happens when we die?"

Lucy's mom looked lovingly at the young girl by her side. She wrapped an arm around her and ran her other hand gently through her daughter's hair.

"I don't know what happens when we die, sweetheart, so I suppose I am one of the people who is okay with not knowing. But I can tell you that I think you are the most important thing to me in the entire world, and in the entire universe, and I feel so lucky to be alive and to have you as my daughter that I am going to do everything I can to help you to lead your very best life right here on earth, which includes asking all sorts of questions about all sorts of things you're curious about. In the meantime, I hope you find as much joy and comfort in being here on the couch with me as I do in being on the couch with you. Because to me, this is one of the very best parts about being alive. How'd I do? Is that a good enough answer?"

"I don't know."

"I don't really know either, love. But I suppose there are some things I want you to decide for yourself as you get older, and this may be one of them. Okay? How about that? Any better?"

"I feel like you didn't really answer it, but I guess I'll just ask you again on my next birthday when I'm older. That feels good on my hair."

Lucy curled up on her mom's lap and closed her eyes. Within a minute, her breathing was slow and deep. *Out like a light*, her mother mused to herself as she carefully reached over and turned off the side table lamp.

*

I'm confused.

Do you want to talk about it?

I never want to talk about it.

Okay.

He did this sometimes, acting as his own therapist. He rarely said things out loud, although sometimes he heard himself. The conversations mainly took place in his head in that infinite landscape of bottomless thought that managed to exist within that relatively narrow diameter of space. The conversations gave him a way to streamline it.

I feel stupid. Like I'm thinking things I don't really feel because I'm not in a proper head space. Like I'm not seeing the forest through the trees because I've only been surrounded by this one tree, so it's all I see. It sounds cliché, but that's how I feel.

It doesn't sound cliché.

He appreciated the support of his feelings.

What kind of tree is it?

I can't tell. Something that stays green year round. It's big, and really tall, and the trunk is so dark it's almost black. But it's not. It's just a deep brown.

It sounds beautiful.

It is.

It was, in fact, a beautiful tree.

And it smells incredible.

What does it smell like?

Clean. Like you know you're breathing in something pure just by breathing around it. I hate hearing myself say this out loud. It all sounds so trite.

It sounds like a tree I would like very much.

Yeah, I think you would.

His phone rang. He ignored it, then intentionally put it on silent. A moment later, he turned it off entirely.

Sorry about that.

No problem.

I can feel disconnected when I don't have my phone near me. Although sometimes I actually feel more connected when it's off.

I don't think you're the only person who feels that way.

No, I don't imagine that I am.

He was distracted. He looked out the window. A small bird pecked at the pane. He was not someone who easily recognized one bird from another, nor did he particularly care about the species in general. Though he did like this bird. It had a spunky personality. And just like that, the bird flew away.

Do you like birds?

It was the therapist who asked.

I don't feel that strongly about them one way or the other.

They say humans don't respond as strongly to birds because we cannot relate to their faces on an emotional level, or something along those lines.

221

Huh.

What is it?

I'm just thinking about that. It's not a concept I've thought about before. That you need to be able to understand someone's face on an emotional level in order to be able to connect to them.

He was quiet for a long time.

Do you want to talk about what it is you're thinking about?

I'm still thinking about the bird thing. I'm not sure I agree, is all.

What do you not agree with?

I'm not sure I need to read the emotions on someone's face in order to connect with them. That's all I was thinking.

And yet, you're not that into birds.

Right.

He chuckled. He always appreciated a slight poke of good-humoredness at his expense.

Anyway.

You were talking about only seeing the one tree.

Right. I feel like I'm blinded by the one tree because it's the only tree in my line of sight.

That makes a lot of sense.

Right.

Right.

It's just that, I don't know. I like the tree. I like being around it.

It does sound like a really nice tree.

It is really nice.

He closed his eyes and took a deep inhalation. It was more of an inward sigh, but he unexpectedly caught the scent of the tree.

I don't even know how I came across it. I wasn't looking for it. It was just around this one bend a few hundred yards off the trail. I couldn't stop looking at it, and so I walked over to it. I looked up and couldn't see through the top branches. The green was so dense and the tree was so tall. The air smelled so good. I couldn't stop looking at it. I sound like a broken record.

You don't sound broken to me.

I feel broken.

How?

This is where I always get stuck. I'm off the trail, which feels wrong. But I'm around this tree, which feels right. And so I'm torn between two things that feel right.

People have been in worse situations.

Yeah. It's just….

He trailed off.

What's that?

I don't know. It's like, at least the path is a path which goes somewhere. Or just goes at all.

And the tree just stays there.

Yeah. Something like that.

Is that how you see the tree? As something that is not a part of the path?

I can't tell. It feels like I want it to be part of the path, but I know that it's not.

How do you know that?

I don't know.

Is it possible that it's already become a part of your path?

That is possible.

The bird was back at the window again. The man watched it. She pecked a few meager pecks and then was off again. He wondered why he decided it was a she. He did not in fact know if it were male or female.

I do love to hike.

Yeah?

The man was pretty sure it was the therapist who spoke first, but he couldn't be certain.

Yeah. It's something I enjoy by myself. I do it a fair amount. One of the many perks of having a relatively flexible schedule.

I like hiking, too.

I have a few favorite places I like to go, and I never cease to be amazed how they look different every time. This one trail in particular. I swear they've rerouted it every time I go.

Rerouted it how? Like it just goes a different way, or you get lost?

It's never quite clear. I always feel lost while I'm on it, but I always seem to end up back at my car.

Huh.

It's the strangest thing.

*

She quietly peeled back the covers and slipped out of bed. Her husband, unruffled and facing away, maintained his steady breathing, a slight purr escaping his parted lips every fourth or fifth breath.

It was the third night that week that she'd been unable to fall back asleep after using the bathroom, so it didn't take her long to figure out what to do, which was to pull up the nearby armchair and watch her husband sleep. She placed it about a foot or so from the bed, stretched her legs out before her at an angle such that they rested easily on the bedframe, crossed one leg over the other, and rested her hands across her lap, her fingers loosely intertwined.

The first night she woke and failed to fall back asleep she busied herself, first making a snack of carrots and hummus, then reading on the couch, then watching the tail end of a pre-recorded episode of her favorite murder mystery, and then, some two hours later, heading back to the bedroom to attempt to fall back asleep. It was then that she caught sight of her husband's face. She was surprised, nearly taken aback at the man she saw sleeping. At the man she had slept beside for forty some odd years whose face suddenly looked like the face of an angel.

She was not one to throw the word out in casual conversation as in *ah yes, I know Carol, she's an angel.* In fact, she rarely used the word at all. But at that moment when she saw the face of her husband, a face she knew better than her own, the unsought thought that swept into and through her mind before lodging itself in the base of her heart was *that is the face of an angel.*

She knew not a moment later that it had to do with his vulnerability. His mouth and face relaxed, his curled position. He was just so vulnerable. And that is when she decided to pull up the armchair, sit down, and watch her husband sleep.

She never thought she would be in one of those relationships where each partner had their own side of the bed, but it was only a mere few months into their marriage that she assumed the side by the patio doors and her husband, that closest to the closet. It was an easy evolution.

Yet only in watching her husband sleep did she realize their arrangement had never allowed her the opportunity to see his face as he slept. He always slept on his side facing out. *Truly, the face of an angel.*

She was surprised to wake the second night. Again, she made a small snack, but after the snack, she went back to the bedroom, pulled up the armchair and watched her husband sleep for close to two hours. She was not distracted as she watched. She did not use the bathroom nor get up to walk around, to stretch her legs. She just watched. Same position, her legs crossed before her and at an angle resting on the bedframe.

Upon waking tonight, she wondered if she were not beginning to wake up on purpose. She had experienced occasional bouts of insomnia years ago when the kids were home - mainly, if one of the kids were going through a tough spell or had something big coming up. And she had woken a few times when her husband had his own bouts of insomnia, he a far lighter sleeper. But for the better part of her life, she had been a sound sleeper. A great sleeper, one might say. She loved sleeping, and it was usually only a matter of minutes after her head hit the pillow before she was out. But this week, she was up. And given how much pleasure she took in watching her husband sleep the first two times, she was all but ready to heat up some popcorn this go round.

I wish I had known him when he was a boy. It wasn't something she though often, but it occurred to her from time to time. Her mother-in-law always told her how easy he had been, how sweet he had always been to his sisters, how he had loved glow-in-the-dark star stickers. He looked sweet enough in his childhood photos, but watching him sleep now, she nearly ached for it. Ached to go back in time and watch him walk to school, watch him get his hair cut by his dad, watch his first kiss, watch him learn how to drive a car, even watch him the first time he slept with a girl. She could only imagine how nervous he must have been. He could be so shy. *God, I love him.* She instinctively grabbed at her heart with her right hand. This was not news to her. She had always been keenly aware of how much she loved her husband. It was a heart-grabbing with which she was familiar.

He let out another purr and she naturally looked at his mouth. *He has the best laugh.* His laugh was what got her when they first met. They ended up seated next to one another in the campus dining hall and she was telling him about her day. She had not meant to be funny, but at some point, she began to describe an encounter with a stranger at the local pharmacy. The stranger had held up a lesser-known brand of toothpaste and asked her if she had tried it. She said no, she liked to stick to name brands for her toothpaste. She was about to continue on with the story when the guy she was talking to in the dining hall, the man she now watched sleep, burst into laughter. He laughed so hard a morsel of his salad shot onto her shirt, which sent him reeling even more. Then he just couldn't stop. She liked laughing and thought of herself as having a good sense of humor, but his laughter got her going so hard that day. She laughed almost as hard as he did. Almost. But as much as she laughed and as often as her husband has since told her how he loves her laugh, she knows his laugh is better. It just is. It makes everything just a little bit funnier.

If he watches me sleep, I wonder what kinds of things he thinks about me. She adjusted the armchair and scooted a little bit closer. She gently tossed her long braid over her shoulder and leaned in so that she was only a foot or so away from his face - close enough to study his lines and features but not so close that she might wake him in that way that one often does when someone can sense that they're being watched. She examined his crow's feet, the crisscross of the lines, how this one came to be and that one slanted in that way, and how this one made sense given what his face looked like when he smiled and how that one was in alignment with the shape his eyebrows took when confused or focused. It all made sense, and yet, it was all a surprise.

She could also see how, if viewed a certain way, his face could look grotesque, almost like that of a monster, but the thought of it alone made her smile because he would make a terrible monster. He was far too silly. He wouldn't even be able to make it through the fum of fee-fi-fo-fum without bursting into laughter. And again, she instinctively grabbed at her heart, this time her belly also sinking, her face almost a slight indication of anguish. *God, I love him.* She

sometimes feared she loved him too much. Not
feared, per se, but - the sense that she could
wrap her arms and legs around him and
consume him, a gesture she took with him from
time to time over the decades when he least
expected it, like while reading the paper or
watching a game on TV or doing some sort of
paperwork at the table. She would come over
and, facing him, wrap her body entirely around
him, staying like that for a good minute or two
before releasing him. And for his part, he nearly
always stopped what he was doing to let her
consume him. They rarely spoke in those
moments.

The urge this time was less to wrap herself
around him and more to lie down facing him,
her body mere millimeters away yet perfectly
contoured to his shape. Where his knees bent,
her knees followed; where his lips parted, hers
equally part. A mirror image but in female
form. She resisted, however, not wanting to risk
waking him. She knew how precious this
moment was. And there was no telling if it
would happen again. There was no telling if she
would again wake and again be unable to fall
back asleep on a night when her husband was

wearing the very same pajamas with his body in this exact same S-curve with his hands stacked one over the other beneath his cheek in this exact same way with his lips parted at the exact same angle with his chin ever so slightly lifted to the exact same degree. Nor would he ever be this age again. This exact age at this exact moment, this exact minute, this exact second, and this exact quantum something or other. *The sciences never were my strong suit. I was always more of an art-type girl, but I might get it now. I might get what some of that quantum stuff was about.* And in that moment, it was as if all of quantum theory suddenly flooded through her and made perfect sense.

*

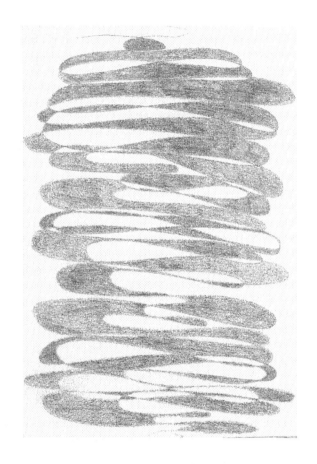

song suggestion: *Water*, Spooky and the Bear

239

a dream in three parts: part three

as she was
holding it up,
perhaps talking about it,
I said that I dreamt
of elephants often.
that there were a few animals
who frequently showed up
in my dreams.
elephants
wolves
bear
moose.
it seems
there may have been
a fifth, though
I do not yet recall.
on waking
I found interesting
their plural forms,
some the same both
singular and plural.
I realize now
it was
the first time
they all
appeared
in
the same dream.

Perhaps:

see what happens if you: walk with agency.
see what happens if you: walk with strength.
see what happens if you: walk with grace.
see what happens if you: try all three at once.

When you go forth, see what happens if you take
all of you there.

I sometimes think if the world only existed in light that the planet would explode. That at some point, the light would become unsustainable and burst. She requires the recovery and rebirth inherent in the dark, the night, the rest, the womb.

It seems the trick is to tap into the magic. Magic is light twinkling in the dark.

It seems this generation of children has the magic about them.

I believe our most important task is to protect the spirit of children. And by spirit I mean the very essence of every aspect of their unique being. Something about this feels like the beginning of how we will heal. And by we I mean humanity. And by humanity I mean the world.

If you think about it, if you really think about it,
it is possible that you are the embodiment of all
forms of beauty.

Everything and nothing all at once. I'm going with everything.

this is an ode
to a young girl,
a girl who might lead
the exact same life
as the life I have led,
though I think it important
that she lead her life
as her life comes to her and
as she steps to meet it.
and so,
I will let her.
but
there is one thing,
one thing I must insist
she know,
which is that
no matter what happens,
no matter what happens
when you are a child,
and when you are a young girl,
and when you are a young woman,
and when you become a woman,
no matter what happens,
that light will still be there.
it will be on a low simmer
deep in the background
staying safe.

but it is there.
trust that it is there.
because there will come a day,
I promise you,
I promise you,
there will come a day,
a day that at times
may seem very far away, but
there will come a day
when that light
will feel safe
and will know that
it is time
to turn up the heat,
just a little bit at a time
until one day,
before you know it,
that small light,
that was on that low simmer,
deep in that background,
will be a flame.
And that flame,
comfortable with its fire,
will turn up the heat
a little bit more
until one day,
before you know it,

that small light,
that was on that low simmer,
deep in that background,
that became that flame,
will become a torch.

song suggestion: *Taking Over*, Joe Goddard

this is it. it's your life to live. you got this.

I just told you why. because I find you to be quite beautiful, as you are, and it is possible you are just getting started. because you deserve what you would wish for a child, and I receive you as such. because your life up to now has laid the groundwork for you, and I believe you know a thing or two. because every time you cried, you released some of your beauty to the world, and because there is only so much you could have known. because I see your resiliency, and because your beauty overwhelms me. because we are all complicated, and because I am here to recognize all of your greatness. because your life is a spectrum, and that spectrum is stellar which places you among the stars. because we need you to help the math add up, and because your force is a part of the world's rhythm. because I can barely control my emotion and intense desire for you to be a part of humanity's beauty set into motion, and because your timeline allows me to see all of you in perspective. because our forest would be nothing without you in it, and who would I have to laugh with. because we all have our flaws, and I recognize every time you have boldly instigated change in your life. because you deserve self-love and self-respect, and because you deserve to heal. because I stand beside you as you do things in spite of your fears, and because of how you balance between building yourself and allowing for life's humilities. because without your frequency, all of music would suffer, and there are so many who would have no one to tune into. because a dove once told me of your value, and I would like for you to see the herons take flight. because your thoughts astonish me, and because if you don't see how necessary you are to our collective existence, then I got a beef with you. because I allow you to be, and because I want to hold the space for your essence to shine. because your body and soul are continuing to learn how to sync up as you grow into yourself, and because there is a chance you are an angel, the very thought of which takes my breath away. because with each sunset, your heart may skip a beat, reminding you of just how incredible your heartbeat is, and because of course you need to rest at times so that when you love, you may love fiercely. because of your strength, and because of your ability to hold the existence of seeming opposites, both of which make you majestic. because you are no coincidence, and that is enough for me. because each time I picture a feather, I am reminded of your ability to confound in your generosity, and because I deeply value your honesty. because of the new foundation you are creating, and because of the many times when you were so brave. because you have been a part of my dreams, and because this reached you, and so you made everything worthwhile. because this corner of the universe would be empty without you, and because I recognize that you are building your most whole self. because of the beauty of your mind and the fire in your belly, and because of the ways you are learning how to transform energy from stagnancy into beauty. because I have your back, and because I am only interested in lifting you up. because I see your capability, and I love it. because I promise you we are all in this thing together, and because I feel at home as I stand beside you. because I am compelled by you, and because I respect the child within you as I watch you take accountability for your actions. because I believe in the possibility of everything I do not know about you, because of how fired up you are to do great things, and because I trust your intuition. because every time you share your words, I get to hear the voice of your being, and because the cosmos has plenty of room for you to shine your light. because I like it better when you like yourself better, and I am confident the Beatles would agree. because I could go on for days about how much I like it when you get weird, because you have the magic about you, and because you've come so much further than you think. because I value all of your good decisions, and because I see how much power you have. because I believe you are fantastic, and because I choose to let the magic about you be magical. because you are not a robot, and so as dark things arise from time to time, I wish you moments of beauty that I ask you to receive. because I can still see your light twinkle, because you are my muse, and because when I think of the beauty of one's soul, I think of you. because you are everything, and because when you go forth, I want all of you there. because your spirit deserves protection and nurturance for the sake of humankind, and because each time you step into your evolution, you take further ownership of yourself. because of how much you give and how you allow yourself to receive, and because you deserve a life filled with all forms of beauty. and because I

see your flame on that low heat as it stays safe,
and because I see that flame as it slowly turns up
the heat and becomes comfortable with its own
fire, and because I see that flame as it turns up
the heat a little more until, before we both know
it, I am being guided by your light.

s
o
n
g
s
u
g
g
e
s
t
i
o
n

Live Your Life (feat. Rihanna), T.I.

Overture

Looking for Little Egypt

Wired ...

It is Jester it is

Main

Bloodlines

Feeling Bright (First Avon Version) (Edit)

Coming Back Around (Edit)

Nineteen Dances

Promised Rhapsody — Original Mix

The Fire

Over

Oh no car your Space whale

Answers To — Original Mix

Mysteria

Runaway

Something Human

Whask

Everything — Original Mix

Taking over

Love Your Life (First Bloom)

go from here.

thank you, so many more

.

269

Made in the USA
Columbia, SC
13 November 2021

48853500R00169